I didn't know that some plants grow in midair

© Aladdin Books Ltd 1998
Produced by
Aladdin Books Ltd
28 Percy Street
London W1P 0LD

First published in the United States in 1998 by
Copper Beech Books,
an imprint of
The Millbrook Press
2 Old New Milford Road
Brookfield, Connecticut 06804

Concept, editorial, and design by
David West Children's Books

Designer: Robert Perry
Illustrators: Myke Taylor – Wildlife Art Ltd.,
Jo Moore

Printed in Belgium
All rights reserved
5 4 3 2 1

Library of Congress Cataloging-in-Publication Data
Llewellyn, Claire.
Some plants grow in midair and other amazing facts about the rainforest /
by Claire Llewellyn ; illustrated by Mike Taylor.
p. cm. — (I didn't know that—)
Includes index.
Summary: Explains why rainforests are shrinking, how their wildlife is
endangered, and why they and their wildlife are important.
ISBN 0-7613-0714-1 (lib. bdg.). — ISBN 0-7613-0644-7 (trade : hc.)
1. Rain forest ecology—Juvenile literature. [1. Rain forest ecology. 2. Ecology.]
I. Taylor, Mike, ill. II. Title. III. Series.
QH541.5.R27L58 1998   97-41608
577.34—dc21   CIP AC

I didn't know that some plants grow in midair

Claire Llewellyn

COPPER BEECH BOOKS
BROOKFIELD, CONNECTICUT

I didn't know that

Introduction

Did *you* know that the rafflesia is the biggest flower in the world? ... that chimpanzees get food with stones and twigs? ... that the arrow-poison frog's bright colors mean "keep away?"

Discover for yourself amazing facts about rain forests, from their spotted cats to their towering trees – and find out what we can do to ensure their future.

 Watch for this symbol that means there is a fun project for you to try.

 Is it true or is it false? Watch for this symbol and try to answer the question before reading on for the answer.

I didn't know that

it can rain every day in a rain forest. Tropical rain forests grow in places where the weather is so hot and sticky and there's a rainstorm nearly every day. The warm, wet weather is perfect for plants – they just grow, and grow, and grow!

SEARCH & FIND Can you find two monkeys? FIND & SEARCH

Rain forest areas

Tropical rain forests are found near the *equator* in the warmest parts of the world. The largest is the Amazonian rain forest in South America; it's almost 30 times bigger than the U.K.

! In an equitorial rain forest it rains at the same time every day.

 True or false?
Rain forest plants rot in the rain.

Answer: **False**
Rain forest plants don't become soggy in the rain. Their leaves are tough and shiny, and have *drip tips* that make drainpipes for the rain.

To see what happens in a rain forest, put a plastic bag over a houseplant. Leave it in a warm place for a week. As the plant gives off water, the bag begins to mist until water "rains" down the sides.

Squirrel monkey

7

Tallest trees in emergent layer

The trees' branches spread out to form a *canopy* over the forest. Birds, monkeys, and other animals live up here, flying, leaping, or swinging from branch to branch.

Canopy

SEARCH & FIND

Can you find five jaguars?

FIND & SEARCH

It is damp and shady below the canopy. Small trees and huge ferns grow here. Large flowers show up in the gloom.

Understory

Shrub layer

I didn't know that

the world's tallest trees grow in rain forests. Some rain forest trees are up to 260 feet high – about twice as high as most church spires. They grow this tall to reach the sunlight, which gives them the *energy* they need to survive.

 True or false?

Rain forest trees have very long roots.

Answer: **False**

Rain forest trees have short roots because the soil is poor and contains few nutrients. To hold up the trees, strong supports called buttress roots grow around the base of the trunk.

Sword-billed hummingbird

I didn't know that

hummingbirds drink from flowers.
Hummingbirds are tiny American birds
that feed on rain forest flowers. They hover in
midair, beating their wings very fast. They put their
long beaks inside the petals and suck up the *nectar*.

Butterflies have long tongues to reach the nectar in flowers.

The toucan uses its long beak to reach fruit at the end of a branch.

The quetzal feeds on the fruit of the avocado tree. It spreads the trees seeds by spitting out the fruit's hard pit. The pit grows where it falls.

SEARCH & FIND
Can you find the stick insect?

 To grow an avocado pit pierce it with toothpicks, and hang it on a jar with the base of the pit in water. When roots grow, plant it in *compost* and put it in a sunny place.

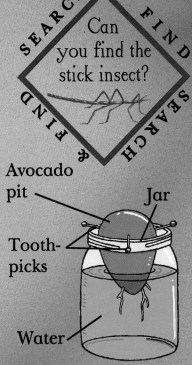

Avocado pit

Jar

Tooth-picks

Water

True or false?
The sloth eats its meals upside down.

Answer: **True**
The sloth lives in South America. This slow-moving animal spends its life hanging upside down from the trees, where it feeds on buds, fruits, and leaves.

Large wandering spiders creep through the trees, hunting for frogs, lizards, and snakes. They even catch birds as they sit on their nests.

Leopard

 True or false?
Rain forest eagles are the biggest in the world.

Answer: **True**
The huge harpy eagles of South America stand about three feet tall. They sail over the canopy, using their massive claws and strong, hooked beaks to catch birds, monkeys, and sloths.

The emerald tree boa eats tree frogs and their eggs. It has no trouble climbing a tree. When it wants to rest, the snake coils itself around a branch.

SEARCH & FIND

Can you find the leaf insect?

FIND & SEARCH

I didn't know that leopards ambush their prey. Leopards live in the forests of Africa and Asia, and hide silently in the trees. As soon as an animal passes below, these big cats drop down and kill their prey.

Water chevrotain

! Hordes of army ants attack small animals on the forest floor.

I didn't know that

some plants grow in midair.

Some rain forest plants don't grow on the ground. To get extra sunlight, these *epiphytes* perch high on the branches of trees, and take in water from the air.

SEARCH & FIND & SEARCH & FIND Can you find ten wasps?

In garden centers you can buy plants that were originally grown from rain forest plants. Go to a garden center and see how many rain forest plants you can find.

The spectacular rafflesia is the largest flower in the world – and the smelliest! Its foul odor helps to attract flies, which then spread the flower's pollen.

True or false? Some plants eat flies.

Answer: **True**

Pitcher plants have slippery, vase-shaped leaves that give off a sugar-sweet smell. When an insect lands on the plant, it slips down into the vase. There, it drowns and dissolves in a juice, which the plant slowly drinks.

An Amazon water lily's leaf is strong enough to hold a child.

Tarzan of the Apes tells the story of a boy who is brought up by apes in the rain forest, and even learns to swing through the trees.

Orangutan

I didn't know that

old men climb through the trees. The word *orangutan* is a *Malay* word that means "old man of the forest." Orangutans are rare apes that live in Southeast Asia. Their strong arms and hooked fingers help them move through the trees.

! On the ground, gibbons lift their long arms to help them to balance.

Chimpanzees are small apes in the forests of Africa. They are clever animals, and have learned to use simple tools, such as stones to smash nuts, and twigs to catch termites inside their nests.

The South American spider monkey has a strong, muscular tail which it uses to hang from the trees. It can even pick nuts with it!

 True or false?
Gorillas are fierce animals.

Answer: **False**
Gorillas are not fierce. This is a myth that some movies have helped to spread. They are peaceful animals unless disturbed or threatened. They live in family groups in the African rain forest, feeding on fresh fruit and leaves.

17

I didn't know that

some trees grow on stilts.

Mangrove trees grow in places where rain forests meet the sea. They have strong roots like stilts, which support them as they stand above the muddy *swamps* and the swirling, salty tides.

SEARCH & FIND Can you find the mangrove snake? FIND & SEARCH

Saltwater crocodiles live around the swamps of Southeast Asia. They are the world's largest crocodiles, and can measure 26 feet from snout to tail. They are strong enough to attack and kill young tigers!

True or false?
Some fish can climb trees.

Answer: **True**

At low tide, mudskipper fish leave the swamp, prop themselves up on their strong, fleshy fins, and crawl over the mud. The fish carries water in its gills to breathe, and even climbs trees in search of food.

Mudskipper

This muddy swamp is full of leaves and tiny plants and animals. At low tide, a huge army of fiddler crabs comes out to feed on them.

Meat-eating piranhas live in the rain forest rivers.

I didn't know that

some frogs are poisonous.

The arrow-poison frog's skin contains a strong poison that deters its enemies from eating it. The frog warns its enemies of this deadly weapon by being brightly colored, meaning "keep away."

SEARCH & FIND & SEARCH & FIND

Can you find eight frogs?

Birds with bright colors are easier to spot in the dark, shady forest. Male manakins have wonderful blue, green, and yellow feathers, which help them attract a mate.

The eyed silkmoth has large, scary eyespots on its wings. When it is threatened by a hungry bird, the moth flashes its eyespots to confuse the enemy, and gives itself time to escape.

! A gaboon viper's speckly skin hides it on the forest floor.

Flying fox

I didn't know that

foxes fly in the jungle. The large
fruit bats of Southeast Asia are also
known as flying foxes. At night,
they fly long distances to feed
on ripe forest fruits.

SEARCH & FIND
Can you find ten fireflies?
FIND & SEARCH

True or false?
Snakes can hunt in the dark.

Answer: **True**
Some snakes, such as the bushmaster, have holes called pits in their head. These work like heat-detectors, picking up the warmth of nearby animals, which the snake then attacks in the dark.

Prey

African bush babies can see in the dark. They have huge eyes like saucers. These trap the light, so the animals can leap from tree to tree at night!

Heat-sensitive pit

Bushmaster

I didn't know that

people live in the rain forest.
People have lived in the rain forest for
thousands of years. They know all about
the different plants and animals and can
use them for food, *fuel*, clothes, and
other everyday needs.

SEARCH & FIND
Can
you find
the returning
hunter?
FIND & SEARCH

Korowai tribesmen,
Indonesia

Rain forest people are often
short and slightly built. Scientists
believe that they have
developed like this
to suit their
surroundings. A
small person can
climb trees and
move through the
forest more easily.

There are so many rivers in a rain forest that the easiest way to travel is by boat. Canoes are made by hollowing out tree trunks and logs.

Hunting in the forest takes practice, time, and skill. Hunters kill animals using either long *blowpipes* or bows and arrows. They dip the tips of their darts and arrows into deadly poisons that they make from animals and plants.

I didn't know that

rain forests are in danger.
People are cutting down huge areas
of the rain forest. They sell the trees
and then burn the land to clear it
for cattle, crops, and *mines*.

As the trees are cut down, animals lose their homes and their numbers begin to shrink. There are only about 150 golden lion tamarins left in the wild, and they may soon become *extinct*.

SEARCH & FIND
Can you find the parrot?

True or false?
Tourists can help the rain forest.

Answer: **True**
Small groups of tourists can help the rain forests. "*Eco-tourists*" respect the forests and want to learn about the animals and plants. The money they pay is used to protect endangered animals.

Planes drop "bombs" of seeds on the rain forests to resow them.

I didn't know that

rain forest plants save lives. Rain forest plants fight off harmful *pests* by producing special chemicals. Scientists now use these chemicals in medicines to fight disease. A quarter of our medicines come from rain forest plants.

 A lot of food we eat originally came from a rain forest. Go to the grocery store and try and find some rain forest food.

Rubber trees grow in tropical rain forests. The trees contain a milky *sap* called latex, which is used to make rubber. People gather the latex by making deep cuts in the bark.

The rain forests are known as the lungs of the world because they balance and freshen our air. Like all plants, the huge forests take in carbon dioxide from the air and give out oxygen – the gas we all need to survive.

Carbon dioxide in

Oxygen out

Scientists use rock-climbing equipment to explore the towering forests.

Glossary

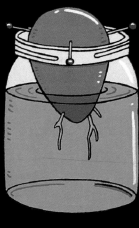

Blowpipe
A hollow tube used by hunters to blow poisoned darts.

Canopy
The top layer of a rain forest, made up of the leaves and branches of the tallest trees.

Compost
A nourishing soil made from decayed plants.

Drip tip
The long point at the end of a leaf.

Eco-tourist
A tourist who wishes to support and observe the natural world.

Energy
The strength to live and grow. Rain forest trees make the Sun's energy into sugars for growth.

Epiphyte
A plant that grows on another plant. An epiphyte uses the other plant as a support, but does not harm it.

Equator

An imaginary line around the middle of the earth, halfway between the north and south poles.

Extinct

An animal is extinct when it no longer lives on the earth.

Fuel

A material, such as wood or coal, that we burn to produce heat or power.

Malay

The language of Malaysia in Southeast Asia.

Mine

Where coal or other materials are dug from the Earth.

Nectar

The sweet liquid inside flowers, which attracts insects, birds and bats.

Pest

A small animal that harms or destroys plants.

Sap

The juice that carries food around inside a plant.

Swamp

Soft, wet, muddy land.

Index